FASCINATING FACTS

EARTH

BY M. J. YORK

childsworld.com

Published by The Child's World®
1980 Lookout Drive • Mankato, MN 56003-1705
800-599-READ • www.childsworld.com

Photographs ©: Micheal Quirk/iStockphoto,
cover (globe), 1 (globe), 2, 7; NASA, cover (Earth),
1 (Earth), 4, 24; iStockphoto, cover (Earth's core),
cover (scale), cover (compass), 1 (Earth's core), 1
(scale), 1 (compass), 3, 6, 8–9, 9, 10, 11, 12–13, 14,
16–17, 18, 19, 21, back cover (astronaut); Tomas
Ragina/iStockphoto, cover (thermometer),
1 (thermometer), 16; Shutterstock Images, 5,
13; Jae Young Ju/iStockphoto, 15, back cover
(satellite); Sepp Friedhuber/iStockphoto, 20

ISBN 9781503844650 (Reinforced Library Binding)
ISBN 9781503846234 (Portable Document Format)
ISBN 9781503847422 (Online Multi-user eBook)
LCCN 2019957695

Printed in the United States of America

ABOUT THE AUTHOR

M. J. York is a children's author
and editor living in Minnesota.
She loves learning about all
kinds of fascinating facts.

CONTENTS

INTRODUCTION

The Blue Marble. The Third Rock from the Sun. The Goldilocks Planet. All of these describe Earth, the only planet we know that has life. Everything on Earth is just right. It is close enough to the sun but not too close. It has enough water but not too much. Here are some all-around fascinating facts about the planet we call home.

Earth is about 8,000 miles (13,000 km) in **diameter**. It **orbits** the sun in just over 365 days. It takes just under 24 hours to rotate on its **axis**. About 71 percent of Earth is covered in oceans, and from space it looks like a blue ball with white swirls. ▶

Earth is a rocky planet. From surface to center, it has four main layers. The crust is the solid, thin layer on the surface of the planet. It is broken into large pieces called plates. These plates are always moving over the mantle. Below, in the mantle, the rocks are mostly solid at the top but more and more melted at greater depths. The outer core is extremely hot and molten. The inner core is just as hot, but the metals are solid.

▼

INNER CORE

OUTER CORE

MANTLE

CRUST

From orbit high above the planet to deep within its core, Earth is amazing!

CHAPTER ONE

All about Earth

Earth's name is unusual. The solar system's other planets are named for Greek or Roman gods and goddesses. The word *earth* is German. It just means "the ground."

Earth is the only planet in the solar system with exactly one moon. But sometimes it picks up temporary **satellites**. Asteroids or large rocks may orbit it for a short time.

The moon is actually made from a piece of Earth! Scientists think that billions of years ago, a big rock smashed into Earth. A chunk of the planet broke off, becoming the moon. ▶

6

People standing at the equator are moving faster than people near the poles. This is because a point on the equator must go farther in one spin than a point near the globe's top. ▶

Earth's rotation is slowing down! **Friction** from ocean tides slows the planet's spin. But the planet is not about to stop! It slows about an extra 1.4 milliseconds every 100 years.

Weighty Matters

Earth is the **densest** planet because it has lots of heavy metals, such as lead and uranium. Earth has the highest **gravity** of any rocky body in the solar system. Denser areas have higher gravity.

Earth is not actually a sphere! It has a bulge at the equator and is a little flatter at the poles. Because Earth's axis is tilted, gravity and other forces do not balance out equally. Water and earth get pushed into the bulge.

7 miles per second

You have to travel 7 miles (11 km) per second to escape Earth's gravity ◄ and launch into space!

People weigh less at the equator than at the poles. The bulge at the equator means people there are farther from the center of Earth. Gravity pulls less on them. The weight loss is about .5 percent. If a person weighs 100 pounds (45 kg) at the poles, then he or she would lose about .5 pounds (.2 kg) at the equator.

People need gravity to stay healthy. ▶ For each month astronauts spend in space, they lose 1 percent of their bone density. Bone density is a measure of the amount of minerals packed into bones.

Older Than Dirt

Scientists think Earth is made of the sun's leftovers. The sun formed from a cloud of dust and gas. After the sun formed, gravity pulled the remaining dust and gas together into planets. At first Earth was just a rocky ball. Then gravity separated it into layers—dense metal at the core and lighter elements toward the surface.

The oldest rocks known to science are in northern Quebec in Canada. They are almost as old as the planet! They could be as old as 4.28 billion years. Earth is 4.54 billion years old.

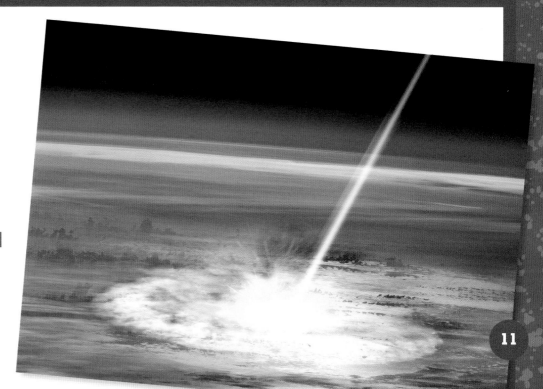

One of the oldest Earth rocks was found on the moon! Astronauts ▲ brought it back to Earth in 1971. Scientists think it is four billion years old. The rock likely launched into space when a meteor hit Earth. Then the rock landed on the moon.

Everyone is made of stardust. About 40,000 tons (36,000 metric tons) of dust from space fall on Earth every year. The dust becomes part of everything on the planet.

CHAPTER TWO

Metals and Magnets

Earth's inner core is not nearly as old as the planet. The inner core has only been solid for about one to 1.5 billion years.

The inner core is about as hot as the liquid outer core, but it is solid. This is because the extreme pressure keeps the iron from melting. Some scientists call the inner core a plasma that acts like a solid.

Together, the inner and outer ▶ core are about twice the size of the moon!

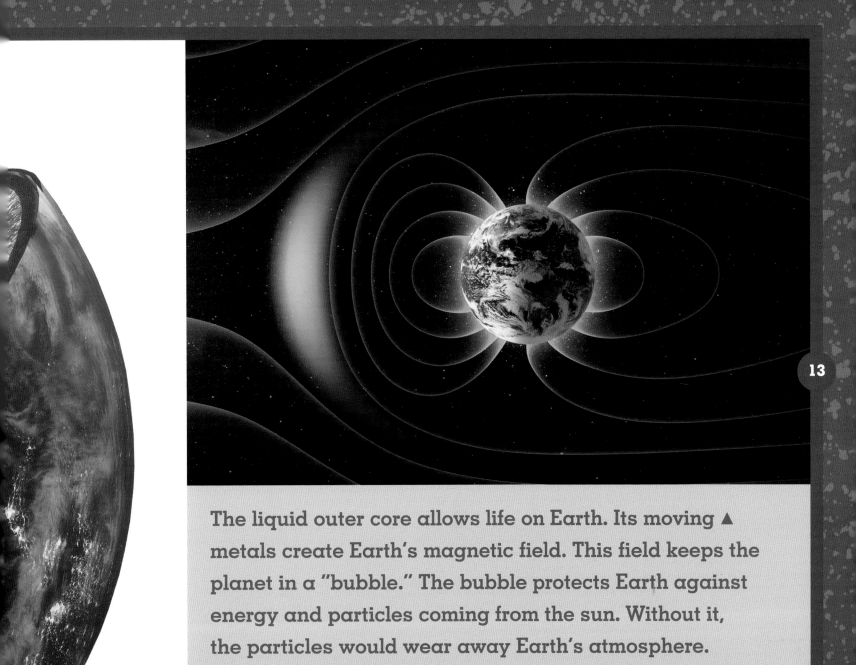

The liquid outer core allows life on Earth. Its moving ▲
metals create Earth's magnetic field. This field keeps the
planet in a "bubble." The bubble protects Earth against
energy and particles coming from the sun. Without it,
the particles would wear away Earth's atmosphere.
Everything on Earth would die without the atmosphere.

Out in the Magnetic Field

The poles are always wandering. The magnetic pole closest to Earth's geographic North Pole is moving about 25 miles (40 km) every year. In a few decades, it will be in Siberia instead of North America.

The magnetic pole sometimes ▶ flips! North becomes south and south becomes north. It takes a few hundred or a few thousand years to finish reversing. During this time, compass needles would point in all directions. This has happened a few hundred times in Earth's history.

There is an area where the magnetic field is weakening. This area stretches across the south Atlantic from Chile to Zimbabwe. The field is so weak that satellites do not fly there. Too much radiation gets through and could damage their instruments.

▼

The magnetic field has weakened 10 percent since the 1800s. But this does not mean it is disappearing. Weakening and strengthening like this has happened throughout Earth's history.

CHAPTER THREE

Extreme Earth

The Atacama Desert in South America is the driest place on Earth. There are places in its center where scientists have never recorded rain.

The wettest place in the world is in India. The village of Mawsynram gets about 39 feet (11.9 m) of rain each year. That is about the height of a telephone pole.

The hottest recorded air temperature on Earth ▶ was 134 degrees Fahrenheit (56.7°C) in Death Valley, California, on July 10, 1913. The coldest recorded temperature was -128.6 degrees Fahrenheit (-89.2°C) on July 21, 1983, in Antarctica.

Antarctica is cold and covered with snow, but it is a desert! Its interior gets only 2 inches (5 cm) of **precipitation** a year. But at the same time, its ice sheets hold 70 percent of Earth's fresh water.

Sometimes sand dunes sing! In certain deserts where it is dry enough, the dunes make a deep moaning sound. Researchers discovered the pitch has to do with the size of the grains of sand. Some dunes can make several tones at once as the sand grains shift.

▼

Under the Sea

Almost all of Earth's water, 97 percent, is in the oceans. The Pacific Ocean is so big that all of Earth's continents could fit in it. ▼

People know very little about the deep ocean. Less than 10 percent of the seafloor has been mapped in detail.

Earth's longest mountain range and tallest mountain are both underwater. The Mauna Kea volcano in Hawaii is taller than Mount Everest if you measure from the base. The longest mountain range runs under the Atlantic and Arctic Oceans. It is called the mid-ocean ridge. It is so long that you could fit the Andes Mountains, Rocky Mountains, and Himalayas in it four times.

GREAT BARRIER REEF ————

1,400 miles

◀ The Great Barrier Reef near Australia is the largest living structure on the planet. It is more than 1,400 miles (2,250 km) long. That is about half the distance from New York City to Los Angeles, California. And the reef is visible from space.

Explosive Earth

A river in the Amazon is hot enough to cook animals. Hot water from deep underground rushes to the surface and joins the river. This leaves a stretch of almost 4 miles (6.4 km) of water that is too hot to touch.

There are exploding lakes in Africa! Volcanic activity under three crater lakes leaves a layer of carbon dioxide in the water. The gas can release into the air suddenly, like when a can of soda explodes.

The hottest and deadliest ▶ lakes are filled with lava, not water. There are eight volcanoes on Earth today that have lava lakes. These do not drain away between eruptions. One is on an island near Antarctica.

Some volcanoes grow glass "hair." The glass is called Pele's hair, named for a Hawaiian goddess. The pale, thin glass fibers form when gas bubbles burst at the surface of lava.

A volcano in Mexico sprang up overnight! In 1943, a big crack appeared in the ground in a farmer's field. By the next day, the new volcano was about 164 feet (50 m) tall. It grew twice as tall in the next week. Within a year and a half, the neighboring villages were covered in lava and ash.

Stromboli Volcano near Italy has been erupting almost nonstop for ▲ 2,000 years. Some people call it the Lighthouse of the Mediterranean because it erupts so frequently.

Glossary

axis (AK-sis) The axis is the imaginary straight line a sphere rotates around. Earth's axis is tilted.

densest (DENSS-est) Something is the densest when it is the thickest or heaviest for its size. Earth is the densest planet in the solar system.

diameter (dy-AM-uh-tur) A diameter is a straight line through a circle or sphere. Earth's diameter is about 8,000 miles (13,000 km).

equator (i-KWAY-tur) The equator is the imaginary circle around Earth that is centered between the two poles. The equator goes around Earth at the planet's widest part.

friction (FRIK-shun) Friction is the force of two objects rubbing together. Friction is slowing Earth's rotation.

gravity (GRAV-i-tee) Gravity is the force that pulls an object of less mass toward an object of more mass. Gravity holds the moon in orbit around Earth.

molten (MOHLT-un) Molten means melted by heat. The metals in Earth's outer core are molten.

orbits (OR-bitz) Something orbits when it circles around something else. The moon orbits Earth.

plasma (PLAZ-muh) Plasma is a state of matter that is not dense and does not hold a shape like a gas but has an electric charge. The sun and other stars are made of plasma.

precipitation (pri-sip-i-TAY-shun) Precipitation is rain, snow, or other types of water that fall to Earth. Deserts get very little precipitation.

radiation (ray-dee-AY-shun) Radiation is a type of energy sent out by the sun. Too much radiation can harm living things and electronics.

satellites (SAT-uh-lites) Satellites are celestial bodies or human-made vehicles that orbit a larger celestial body. Moons are satellites.

To Learn More

In the Library

Drimmer, Stephanie Warren. *Ultimate Secrets Revealed!*
A Closer Look at the Weirdest, Wildest Facts on Earth.
Washington, DC: National Geographic, 2018.

What's Weird on Earth. New York, NY: DK Publishing, 2018.

Woodward, John. *Super Earth Encyclopedia.*
New York, NY: DK Publishing, 2017.

On the Web

Visit our website for links about Earth:

childsworld.com/links

*Note to Parents, Teachers, and Librarians: We routinely verify our Web links to make sure
they are safe and active sites. So encourage your readers to check them out!*

Index